# 2022
# *Cape Cod*
## Restaurants

The Food Enthusiast's
Long Weekend Guide

**Andrew Delaplaine**

*Andrew Delaplaine is the Food Enthusiast.*
*When he's not playing tennis,*
*he dines anonymously*
*at the Publisher's (considerable) expense.*

**James Cubby – Senior Editor**

The Food Enthusiast's
Long Weekend Guide

# *Table of Contents*

# *INTRODUCTION*

Every time I'm in the Hamptons, the thought crosses my mind that "I'd rather be on Cape Cod."

Every time I'm on Cape Cod, I think two things: "Thank God it never turned into the Hamptons" and "Thank God it's still the same."

It's not of course. Nothing ever really is the same. But when you run into old-timers on Long Island, they'll tell you how it was in the Hamptons before the mega-rich moved in and built their monstrously inappropriate mansions, bringing along with them, naturally, their monstrously inappropriate attitudes. The Hamptons with their fancy shops and nightclubs. (Can you ever imagine a NIGHTCLUB on Cape Cod? Not really. Who would ever go to it? I'm not including P-town in this statement—with all the gay people out there, of course they have nightclubs.)

Cape Cod is really one of the great things about America. There's a unique ecosystem or lifestyle or way of life or mindset on the Cape, however you may want to describe it.

The cheesy little stores selling dust collecting souvenirs, the roadside seafood shacks selling fried clams the way they have for decades, the quiet beaches on Nantucket Bay, the shops selling saltwater taffy and other summer goodies—all of it is remarkably the same as it was when my grandmother used to drag us out there from Boston every summer.

It's kinda like the northern version of the Florida Keys. (Though the local people couldn't be more different if they tried—the ones up on the Cape actually read books and know who's President. In the Keys, they couldn't care less.)

Like Key West, Cape Cod, and especially P-town, has been a magnate for artists of every type. If you're lucky, you might be able to catch filmmaker John Waters tooling around town on his weird looking bike.

Just as the Keys are divided into three parts, the Upper, Middle and Lower Keys, Cape Cod goes them one better and is divided roughly into four parts: the Upper Cape, Mid-Cape, Lower Cape and Outer Cape. (Five parts if you count the Islands—Martha's Vineyard, Nantucket and Gosnold.)

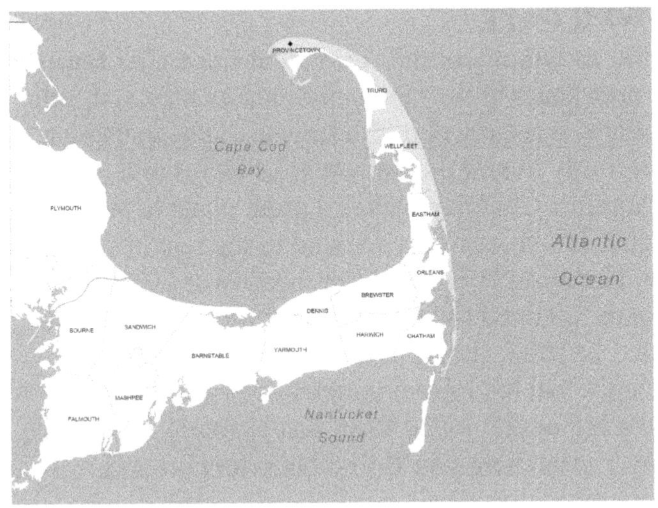


## UPPER CAPE

The Upper Cape runs north to south and is bounded by Buzzards Bay and the Cape Cod Canal. Sandwich takes the honors as the oldest town on the Cape, thus the most historic. Charming Falmouth and its lovely waterfront aren't far away. Wood's Hole, of course, is home to the big oceanographic institute you've probably heard a lot about over the years. Then there's Mashpee, New Seabury, Bourne.

## MID-CAPE

Exactly as the name indicates, Mid-Cape is in the middle of the peninsula, boasting towns like Hyannis (famed for its Kennedy connection), Osterville (where we stayed with grandmother in a whitewashed house), Barnstable Village, Dennis, Yarmouthport, Centerville, West Barnstable, Craigville, Cummaquid, HyannisPort.

## LOWER CAPE

In the geography of the "arm" that Cape Cod forms, this area starts at the elbow and makes its way north. Chatham is the jewel of the Lower Cape, sporting a charmingly quaint downtown area, shops and restaurants. Chatham makes a great place to stay because it's so centrally located to the rest of Cape Cod. Here you'll find Also in the Lower Cape is Orleans, claimed to be the spot where Leif Eriksson landed in 1003. (Long before the lobster roll, he probably had his lobster cooked over a spit with no drawn butter and loved them just as much as we do today.) Also here you'll find Harwichport and Brewster.

The thing that gets me about Leif Eriksson is why in God's name he didn't send his boat back and tell the crew to bring their families. Think of the real estate he could have stolen from the Indians.

## OUTER CAPE

As the "forearm" of Cape Cod moves north, you enter what is called the Outer Cape. On one side you have Cape Cod Bay and on the other the Atlantic. The peninsula becomes quite narrow out here, and you pass through towns like Eastham (not that there's much of a "town" there) and Truro with great views from the cliffs and the Cape Cod Light, before you get to wonderful Wellfleet. (Think "Wellfleet oysters.") This is a great little town I love very much, a civilized respite from the madness of the last stop,

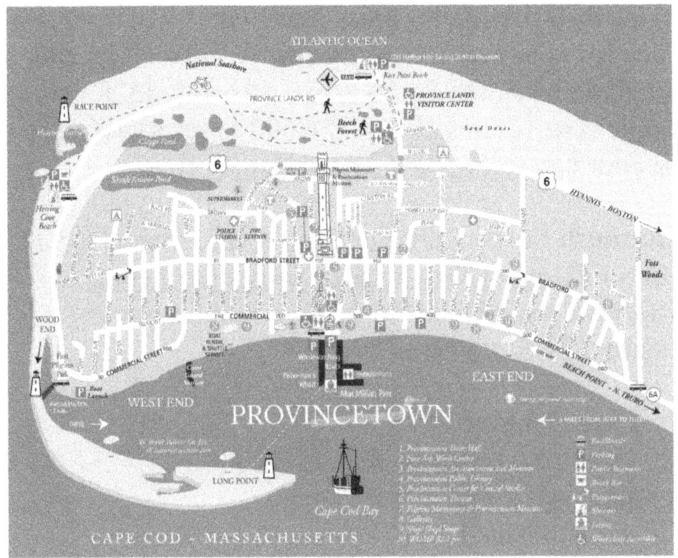


Provincetown, or "P-town" to locals, a sizeable number of whom are gay.

P-town is a world unto its own on Cape Cod. There are dozens of little towns on the Cape you could pick up, move 20 or 30 miles and set down again and nobody would notice anything different. But you couldn't do that with P-town. It's completely unique.

## THE ISLANDS

### Martha's Vineyard & Nantucket

Several Cape Cod harbors have ferries that will take you to Martha's Vineyard.

The **Island Queen** operates out of Falmouth Harbor. Quickest way if you don't have a car. 30-40 minutes from dock to dock. 75 Falmouth Heights Rd, 508-548-4800. www.islandqueen.com/

**Steamship Authority** takes cars over. Must reserve a place for your car. 1 Cowdry Rd, Wood's Hole, and also from 65 South St, Hyannis. 508-495-3278 for people reservations, 508-477-8600 to reserve a place for your car. www.steamshipauthority.com/

**Falmouth Ferry** , 278 Scranton Ave, Falmouth, 508-548-9400. www.falmouthedgartownferry.com/ Offers only service to Edgartown in the summer aboard a 72-foot vessel.

**Hy-Line Cruises**
220 Ocean St, Hyannis, 508-778-2600
hylinecruises.com/
Serves both islands.

**WHEN TO VISIT**

I prefer the slightly off-season Spring and Autumn periods over the high summer season to visit Cape Cod. But then, I can do without most beach activities that if you have a family, you'll want to take advantage of. Kids want to swim. The worst time for me is 4th of July through Labor Day. This is the high summer season. The four weeks before or the four weeks after make the perfect time to visit. The crowds are less, the rates are lower, you can get into the best restaurants without a hassle and the car traffic is reduced to somewhat sane levels, not something you can say in high season.

# *GETTING ABOUT*

You will need a car, pure and simple.
There is bus service along the Cape. Details at www.p-b.com. But once you get into a town, you'll be at the mercy of taxis, which can be expensive, even for short jaunts.
In 2013, a new train service was started (the first since 1959), called the **Cape Flyer**. www.capeflyer.com -- it's a weekend service that runs from Boston's South Street Station Friday-Sunday Memorial Day through Labor Day. Definitely worth checking out if you're going to a certain location and don't plan to travel around the Cape very much.

# *The A to Z Listings*

*Ridiculously Extravagant*
*Sensible Alternatives*
*Quality Bargain Spots*

**28 ATLANTIC**
2173 Massachusetts 28, East Harwick, 508-430-3000
www.wequassett.com/dining#/twenty-eight/
CUISINE: Seafood/American
DRINKS: Full Bar
SERVING: Breakfast & Dinner; open Fri, Sat & Sun
PRICE RANGE: $$$

This elegant waterfront eatery offers an impressive menu of seafood and classic American dishes. The eight-foot windows offer beautiful views of Pleasant Bay. Note: Dress code forbids denim, collarless shirts, shorts and athletic shoes.

**99**
1600 Falmouth Rd, Bell Tower Mall, Centerville, 508-790-8995
14 Berry Ave, West Yarmouth, 508-862-9990
www.99restaurants.com
CUISINE: American
DRINKS: Full bar
SERVING: Lunch & Dinner daily
PRICE RANGE: $$
If you have a bunch of kids, this is the place to bring them. Reasonable prices and good-sized portions. Everything from entree salads, burgers, sandwiches and wraps, steaks and ribs, seafood, chicken and turkey, soups and sides.

**400 EAST**
1421 Orleans Rd #21, Harwich, 508-432-1800
www.the400east.com
CUISINE: American/Italian
DRINKS: Full Bar
SERVING: Lunch, Dinner
PRICE RANGE: $$
This casual tavern offers a menu of American comfort food. Menu favorites include thin crust pizza and fresh ground burgers.

**ABBA**
89 Old Colony Way, Orleans, 508-255-8144
www.abbarestaurant.com
CUISINE: Mediterranean
DRINKS: Full Bar
SERVING: Dinner
PRICE RANGE: $$$
Chef Erez Pinhas hails from Israel, and while he offers some items that reflect this (like falafel in a tahini-amba sauce), it's the Asian influences that produce standout dishes (like the shrimp & lobster pad Thai). This is not a big place, so be prepared to grab a seat at the bar if you have to. The food's worth

it. (Lots of people say this is the best restaurant on the whole Cape, but them there is fightin' words.)

**ALBERTO'S RESTAURANT**
360 Main St, Hyannis, 508-778-1770

www.albertos.net
CUISINE: Italian
DRINKS: Full Bar
SERVING: Lunch, Dinner
PRICE RANGE: $$$
This tried-and-true fine-dining eatery offers a menu of Northern Italian fare. Menu favorites include: Short ribs and Chicken Scaloppini with artichoke hearts. Impressive wine list.

**AMARI BAR AND RESTAURANT**
674 Route 6A, East Sandwich, 508-375-0011
www.amarirestaurant.com
CUISINE: Italian
DRINKS: Full Bar
SERVING: Lunch, Dinner
PRICE RANGE: $$
This welcoming bar and restaurant offers a menu of Italian classics. Menu favorites include: Lobster and seafood over rice, and Broiled Salmon. Live music.

**ANEJO MEXICAN BISTRO & TEQUILA BAR**
188 Main St, Falmouth, 508-388-7631
www.anejomexicanbistro.com
CUISINE: Mexican
DRINKS: Full Bar
SERVING: Lunch, Dinner
PRICE RANGE: $$
This contemporary Mexican eatery offers an ever-changing menu of Tex-Mex favorites and Mexican-style street food. Casual dining on the patio is nice during warmer months. Reservations recommended.

**ARNOLD'S LOBSTER & CLAM BAR**
3580 State Hwy, Eastham, 508-255-2575
www.arnoldsrestaurant.com
CUISINE: Seafood, Ice cream and frozen yogurt
DRINKS: Full Bar
SERVING: 11:30 am – 9:30pm daily
PRICE RANGE: $$
Since 1976 they've been serving a fried lobster tail that consistently draws raves.

**BARLEY NECK INN**
5 Beach Rd, Orleans, 508-255-0212
www.barleyneck.com
CUISINE: Seafood/American
DRINKS: Full Bar
SERVING: Lunch, Dinner
PRICE RANGE: $$$
Located in a historic sea captain's house, this eatery offers four elegant rooms of dining. Favorites include: Lobster chili and Seared Tuna. Great selection of single malt scotches.

**BAXTER'S BOATHOUSE**
177 Pleasant St, Hyannis, 508-775-4490
www.baxterscapecod.com
CUISINE: Seafood
DRINKS: Full Bar
SERVING: Lunch, Dinner
PRICE RANGE: $$
Located in a boathouse built over the water, this restaurant offers a great selection of seafood. Favorites include the clam chowder and the fresh haddock.

**BEACH GRILL AT CHATHAM BARS INN**
297 Shore Rd, Chatham, 508-945-0096
www.chathambarsinn.com
CUISINE: American/Seafood
DRINKS: Full Bar

SERVING: Lunch, Dinner
PRICE RANGE: $$$
Located on the water's edge, this is a favorite spot of local's and tourists. This venue offers an impressive menu of New England fare and panoramic view of the Atlantic and Chatham Harbor. Tasty lobster rolls and signature cocktails.

**BETSY'S DINER**
457 Main St, Falmouth 508-540-0060
https://betsys-diner.business.site
CUISINE: American
DRINKS: No Booze
SERVING: Lunch, Dinner
PRICE RANGE: $
This little retro eatery offers typical American diner fare from meatloaf to breakfast served all day.

**BLACKFISH**
17 Truro Center Rd, Truro 508-349-3399
www.blackfishtruro.com
CUISINE: American
DRINKS: Full Bar
SERVING: Lunch, Dinner
PRICE RANGE: $$$
Located in a former blacksmith shop, this eatery offers delicious seafood dishes and a bustling bar scene. Favorites include: The Bone-in Rib eye steak with truffle butter. Nice selection of wines.

**BLEU**
Mashpee Commons, 10 Market St, Mashpee, 508-539-7907

www.bleurestaurant.com
CUISINE: French
DRINKS: Full Bar
SERVING: Lunch, Dinner
PRICE RANGE: $$
This French eatery offers a fine dining experience with a menu of French bistro classics. Favorites include Salmon over asparagus and sweet potatoes. Nice wine pairings.

**BOBBY BYRNE'S RESTAURANT & PUB**
Rt 6 A Tupper Rd, Sandwich, 508-888-6088
www.bobbybyrnes.com
CUISINE: American
DRINKS: Full Bar
SERVING: Lunch, Dinner
PRICE RANGE: $$

This popular eatery offers a diverse and ample menu of homemade Pub favorites, Mexican fare, burgers, sandwiches and hearty salads. Nice wine selection. This place offers a comfortable dining experience.

**BOG PUB**
618 MacArthur Blvd, Pocasset 508-392-9620
www.thebogtavern.com/
CUISINE: American/Burgers
DRINKS: Full Bar
SERVING: Dinner; closed Mon
PRICE RANGE: $$
This place has a loyal following and one visit will make you a fan. The food is great. They start your dining experience with fresh warm toasted bread and flavored oil. Favorites include the clam chowder and hummus. Great bar selection.

**BOOKSTORE & RESTAURANT**
50 Kendrick Ave, Wellfleet 508-349-3154
www.wellfleetoyster.com
CUISINE: Seafood
DRINKS: Full Bar
SERVING: Lunch, Dinner
PRICE RANGE: $$
This popular eatery offers a great menu of tasty seafood favorites. Great creative cocktail menu.

**BRAX LANDING RESTAURANT**
705 Route 28, Harwich Port, 508-432-5515
www.braxrestaurant.com
CUISINE: Seafood
DRINKS: Full Bar

SERVING: Lunch, Dinner
PRICE RANGE: $$
This popular seafood eatery offers a varied menu including specials like the French Dip sandwich and an impressive wine list. This is also a great choice for Sunday Brunch with classic favorites like Eggs Benny and a delicious selection of desserts.

**BRAZILIAN GRILL**
680 Main St, Hyannis, 508-771-0109
www.braziliangrill-capecod.com
CUISINE: Steakhouse
DRINKS: Full Bar
SERVING: Lunch, Dinner
PRICE RANGE: $$$
This steakhouse offers great all-you-can-eat specials with a salad bar and buffet.

All-you-can-eat churrascaria serves slow-cooked meats carved tableside, with a salad bar & buffet. Great desserts.

**BREWSTER FISH HOUSE**
2208 Main St, Brewster, 508-896-7867
www.brewsterfishhouse.com
CUISINE: Seafood
DRINKS: Full Bar
SERVING: Lunch & dinner; NO RESERVATIONS
PRICE RANGE: $$$
Roasted bone marrow or artisanal meat & cheese platters make a good appetizer here. Seared cod, pan-roasted halibut are good main courses. Also the grilled tenderloin & scallops make a good surf & turf selection (served with a goat cheese potato puree, morels, smoked bacon, spring garlic & Béarnaise). The small cottage is quaint, but note they don't take reservations. (Like the locals, I try to swing by during lunch and skip dinner: easier to get a table.)

**BRITISH BEER COMPANY**
46 Rte 6-A, Sandwich, 508-833-9590
263 Grand Ave, Falmouth, 508-540-9600
412 Main St, Hyannis, 508-771-1776
www.britishbeer.com
CUISINE: American
DRINKS: Full bar
SERVING: Lunch & dinner daily
PRICE RANGE: $$
This is a chain of British style pubs serving a good selection of domestic and international craft beers, as well as a dauntingly large menu serving everything

from soups to salads to main courses. It's like most chains that put out those menus so big that you're bound to find something on it. But each location has its own friendly appeal. Dark woods, lively crowds, good pub fare, and there's music later in the evenings.

**BUBALA'S BY THE BAY**
185 Commercial St, Provincetown 508-487-0773
www.bubalas.com
CUISINE: American
DRINKS: Full Bar
SERVING: Lunch, Dinner
PRICE RANGE: $$
This place is known as having the best fried scallops in Provincetown. This is a great place for people watching and casual dining. Favorites include: Grilled Free-Range Chicken Breast and Lobster & Soul Roulade. Live entertainment.

**BUCA'S TUSCAN ROADHOUSE**
4 Depot Rd, Harwich, 508-432-6900
www.thebogtavern.com/
CUISINE: Italian
DRINKS: Full Bar
SERVING: Dinner daily from 5
PRICE RANGE: $$$
Starters like grilled goat cheese polenta topped with orange fig compote, mussels with garlic & fennel, pan-fried gnocchi. For a main course, go for the Caccuicco (littleneck clams, mussels, calamari, shrimp and catch of the day in a rich tomato sauce). They have other hearty Italian dishes like roasted chicken and garlic, eggplant parm, etc.

**BUCATINO**
7 Nathan Ellis Hwy, North Falmouth, 508-566-8960
www.bucawinebar.com
CUISINE: Italian
DRINKS: Full bar
SERVING: Lunch & Dinner
PRICE RANGE: $$$
Popular Italian eatery focusing on fresh seafood. The fireplace adds a lot of coziness to the atmosphere in this charming eatery. Menu picks: Bucatini Bolognese and Shrimp Ravioli. Large portions. Big bar. Excellent wine list.

**C SALT WINE BAR & GRILLE**
75 Davis Straits, Falmouth (774) 763-2954
www.csaltfalmouth.com
CUISINE: American/French

DRINKS: Full Bar
SERVING: Dinner; closed Tues
PRICE RANGE: $$#
Chef/owner Jonathan Philips welcomes guests to his casual bar and grill. Favorites include: Statler Chicken Breast and Grilled Petite Filet Mignon. Great wine and food pairings from an extensive wine list.

**CAFÉ CHEW**
4 Merchant's Rd, Sandwich 508-888-7717
www.cafechew.com
CUISINE: American
DRINKS: No Booze
SERVING: Breakfast, Brunch & Lunch
PRICE RANGE: $
Friendly café with a menu of American favorites. Popular place for breakfast and lunch with outdoor

seating. Favorites include the California BLT with egg. Children's menu.

**CAFÉ RIVERVIEW**
451 Rt 6A, Sandwich, 508-833-8365
www.riverviewschool.org
CUISINE: American (Traditional)
DRINKS: No Booze
SERVING: Breakfast/Lunch
PRICE RANGE: $
NEIGHBORHOOD: Sandwich
Small cafe with walk up service counter serving American fare with twists like the Asian Chicken wrap. Homemade soups, quiche, and smoothies.

**THE CANTEEN**
225 Commercial St, Provincetown, 508-487-3800
www.thecanteenptown.com
CUISINE: Seafood/Fish & Chips
DRINKS: Beer & Wine Only
SERVING: Lunch, Dinner; closed Mon, Tues, & Wed
PRICE RANGE: $$
A popular eatery of locals and tourists features a great menu of seafood and sandwiches. Favorites include Oyster po'boy sandwich and Clam chowder.

**CAPE SEA GRILLE**
31 Sea Street, Harwich Port, 508-432-4745
www.capeseagrille.com
CUISINE: New American
DRINKS: Full Bar
SERVING: Dinner nightly from 5; bar opens at 4:30.

PRICE RANGE: $$$
Asparagus bisque with salmon; shrimp & pork belly ravioli topped with braised cabbage; duck confit; local oysters on the half shell all make good starters. My favorite entrée here is the pan seared whole lobster with pancetta, grilled asparagus and potatoes. Also the trio of Long Island duck (seared breast, confit leg & seared foie gras with dried cherry sauce). Located in a ramshackle old house, this is the perfect location for food like this.

**CAPTAIN FROSTY'S**
219 Main St, Dennis, 508-385-8548
www.captainfrosty.com
CUISINE: Seafood/Fish & Chips
DRINKS: No Booze
SERVING: Lunch, Dinner
PRICE RANGE: $$
This casual seafood shack offers a delicious selection of fresh seafood and burgers. Indoor and outdoor seating. For dessert there's an ice cream shop attached.

**CAPTAIN KIDD**
77 Water St, Woods Hole, 508-548-8563
www.thecaptainkidd.com
CUISINE: Seafood
DRINKS: Full Bar
SERVING: Lunch, Dinner; closed Sun, Mon & Tues
PRICE RANGE: $$
Great place for outdoor summer dining overlooking the pond. Indoor seating available. Favorites include: Kale salad with shrimp and Fish tacos.

**CAPTAIN PARKER'S PUB**
668 Massachusetts 28, West Yarmouth, 508-771-4266
www.captainparkers.com
CUISINE: Seafood
DRINKS: Full Bar
SERVING: Lunch, Dinner
PRICE RANGE: $$
If you're looking for hearty New England fare and great clam chowder, then this is your place. There are also great meat selections like the prime rib. And I'd be remiss if I didn't mention the bustling bar scene that for years has been luring locals and tourists alike. Follow my lead and arrive early to avoid the crowd.

**CERALDI**
15 Kendrick Ave, Wellfleet, 508-237-9811
www.ceraldicapecod.com

CUISINE: Italian
DRINKS: Full Bar
SERVING: Dinner, Closed Mon & Tues.
PRICE RANGE: $$$
NEIGHBORHOOD: South Wellfleet
Counter seating (comfortable chairs with real backs to them, yes!) surrounds the little kitchen on 3 sides—you can either sit here and watch as the cooks do their thing, or take a table against the walls. They only have 45 seats. This is a modern fine dining restaurant offering a rotating 7-course menu of Italian fare that is made right in front of your eyes. Menu changes daily. Many of the ingredients have been farmed, or in the case of fish, caught just a few miles from the restaurant. Excellent wine pairings. Price is not at all unreasonable for what you get.

**CHAPIN'S RESTAURANT**
85 Taunton Ave, Dennis, 508-385-7000
www.chapinsrestaurant.com
CUISINE: Seafood
DRINKS: Full Bar
SERVING: Lunch, Dinner
PRICE RANGE: $$
This casual eatery offers a menu of coastal classics, pastas, steaks, and a raw bar.
Great place for the entire family. Favorites include: The Cobb Salad. End your meal with a little ice cream served at the window outside.

**CHART ROOM**
1 Shipyard Ln, Pocasset, 508-563-5350
www.chartroomcataumet.com

CUISINE: Seafood
DRINKS: Full Bar
SERVING: Lunch, Dinner
PRICE RANGE: $$$
This popular seafood eatery serves great dishes and the harbor view from the porch is almost as good as the food. Very busy during the summer so be prepared to wait. Regulars come back for the great New England clam chowder and the creative cocktails.

**CHATHAM PIER FISH MARKET**
45 Barcliff Ave, Chatham, 508-945-3474
www.chathampierfishmarket.com
CUISINE: Seafood, Sushi, Seafood Market
DRINKS: No booze
SERVING: Lunch & dinner daily
PRICE RANGE: $$
The lobster rolls here are huge. But here they also have shrimp rolls and scallop rolls, so try one of those

instead. Also has sushi, but the menu on that is somewhat limited (which is probably a good thing).

**CHATHAM SQUIRE**

487 Main St, Chatham 508-945-0945
www.thesquire.com
CUISINE: American
DRINKS: Full Bar
SERVING: Lunch, Dinner
PRICE RANGE: $$

This funky little place has a unique décor of wallpaper made from license plates. The menu is strictly classic pub fare with favorites like Lobster Bisque. Specials change daily. There's usually a wait during season but it's worth it. Occasional live music.

**CHATHAM WINE BAR AND RESTAURANT CHATHAM INN**

359 Main St #2, Chatham, 508-945-1468
www.chathamwinebar.com
CUISINE: Wine Bar/American (New)
DRINKS: Wine
SERVING: Dinner
PRICE RANGE: $$$
NEIGHBORHOOD: Chatham

You can't get much better for a Cape Cod experience than to slide into this lovely charmer nestled off to the side of the Chatham Inn (which is a perfect place to stay, I might just as well say right here). It's got very fine dining in one room (choose from 3 or 4 or 5-course menus), a separate outdoor Bistro menu (Lobster & Corn Chowder) on the patio. And there's also a wine bar inside with a cozy dark atmosphere and fireplace and over 30 wines by the glass to choose from). The "fine dining" option is an upscale eatery with a steak and seafood focused menu. Favorites: Lamb shank; Chilled Watermelon Soup; Scallop Ceviche; Snake River Farms Carpaccio; Chicken & Peaches; Halibut with crispy prosciutto; Lobster tail poached in butter. But these were just samples from the menu last time I visited. Changes often. Lovely wine list. Outdoor patio, as I mentioned earlier.

**CHILLINGSWORTH**
2449 Main St, Brewster, 508-896-3640
www.chillingsworth.com
CUISINE: American/French
DRINKS: Full Bar
SERVING: Dinner
PRICE RANGE: $$$
Located on the 300 year-old Chillingsworth Foster estate, this high-end eatery is known as the Cape's most celebrated restaurant and one of Julia Child's favorite places on the Cape. They offer prix-fix

options with a menu of classic French cuisine. Favorites include: Baked Basil Crusted Atlantic Salmon and Roasted Native Swordfish.

**CIRO & SAL'S**
4 Kiley Ct, Provincetown, 508-487-6444
www.ciroandsals.com
CUISINE: Italian, Seafood
DRINKS: Full Bar
SERVING: Dinner
PRICE RANGE: $$$
This go-to eatery for Northern Italian cuisine attracts fans year-round. Favorites include: Breaded veal cutlet served with spaghetti and Oven roasted salmon with a shrimp reduction sauce over risotto. Great wine cellar.

**CLANCY'S RESTAURANT**
8 Upper County Rd, Dennis Port, 508-394-6661
www.clancysrestaurant.com
CUISINE: Seafood
DRINKS: Full Bar
SERVING: Lunch, Dinner
PRICE RANGE: $$
For 26 years, this restaurant has served excellent seafood-influence American fare. Favorites include Fish & Chips and Chicken Parmesan. The casual eatery offers a dining room and a riverfront patio. Open year-round with creative specials changed daily.

**COBIE'S CLAM SHACK**
3260 Main St, Brewster, 508-896-7021
www.cobies.com
CUISINE: Seafood/Fish & Chips
DRINKS: Full Bar
SERVING: Lunch, Dinner
PRICE RANGE: $$
This casual eatery has been attracting crowds since 1948 for great seafood standards, fish & chips and great burgers. Try the ice cream, it's the best on the Cape.

**THE CORNER STORE**
1403 Old Queen Anne Rd, Chatham, 508-432-1077
www.freshfastfun.com
CUISINE: Sandwiches/Mexican/Bakery
DRINKS: No Booze
SERVING: Breakfast/Lunch/early Dinner
PRICE RANGE: $
NEIGHBORHOOD: Chatham

Great variety of sandwiches, paninis and burritos. Favorites: Buffalo-ranch chicken burrito and Chicken B.L.T. Caesar Salad. Great desserts and cookies.

**COTTAGE STREET BAKERY**
5 Cottage St, Orleans, 508-255-2821
www.cottagestreetbakery.com
CUISINE: Bakery; sandwiches
DRINKS: No
SERVING: Daily 6 am - 5 pm
PRICE RANGE: $
Though the baked goods (cakes, pastries, pies) are the prime draw here, the other food is fine. A great selection of sandwiches and soups (like Hungarian mushroom and carrot cilantro). Salads also fresh and lively.

**THE DAILY PAPER**
644 West Main St, Hyannis, 508-790-8800
www.dailypapercapecod.com
CUISINE: Diner
DRINKS: No Booze
SERVING: Breakfast & Lunch
PRICE RANGE: $
This place packs them in for breakfast 7 days a week. Chef owned and operated; here you'll find they use the freshest products available. Besides the classic breakfast, favorites include Lobster Benedict and Corned Beef Hash. They also have Cape Cod Beer on draught.

**THE DAN'L WEBSTER INN & SPA**
149 Main St, Sandwich, 855-958-0066
www.danlwebsterinn.com
CUISINE: American
DRINKS: Full Bar
SERVING: Breakfast, Lunch, & Dinner
PRICE RANGE: $$
This restaurant is recognized as a Distinguished Restaurant in North America and lives up to its ranking. The Inn serves in four dining rooms, each with a different décor, and the Tavern. Traditional favorites include: Prime Rib & Filet Mignon. Chef's Special Menu is constantly changing. Impressive wine list and cellar.

**DEL MAR**
907 Main St, Chatham, 508-945-9988
www.delmarbistro.com

CUISINE: American
DRINKS: Full Bar
SERVING: Lunch, Dinner
PRICE RANGE: $$$
This charming little spot offers a nice selection of bistro fare and seafood specials. The ambiance is welcoming and there's often live jazz. Favorites include Clams over linguini and their famous thin crust wood fired pizza.

**THE DEN**
697 Main St, Dennisport, 508-258-0805
https://dencapecod.com/
CUISINE: American (New)
DRINKS: Full Bar
SERVING: Lunch & Dinner
PRICE RANGE: $$
NEIGHBORHOOD: Dennis Port
Popular eatery resembling a sports bar – lots of TVs, large horseshoe bar and big open dining space. But the space is more clubby than that, with lots of dark-hued wood accents and a silver-tin type ceiling. Menu picks: Scallops with risotto and Grilled oysters. Nice selection of wines and beers (a great many of them on tap).

**DOCKSIDE RIBS N LOBSTER**
110 School, Hyannis, 508-827-4355
www.thedocksidehyannis.com
CUISINE: Seafood
DRINKS: Full Bar
SERVING: Lunch, Dinner
PRICE RANGE: $$

This popular spot offers scenic waterfront dining with a menu of American classics and seafood dishes. Known for their lobster and ribs, they also serve breakfast standards and award winning fish sandwiches.

**DOLPHIN RESTAURANT**
3250 Main St, Barnstable, 508-362-6610
www.thedolphincapecod.com
CUISINE: Sandwiches
DRINKS: Full Bar
SERVING: Lunch, Dinner
PRICE RANGE: $$
This popular eatery features a menu of American and seafood standards. Favorites include the chicken wrap with blueberries and walnuts and Half tuna sandwich and chowder special.

**DUNBAR TEA SHOP**
1 Water St, Sandwich, 508-833-2485
www.dunbartea.com
CUISINE: Coffee and Tea
DRINKS: Beer and Wine Only
SERVING: Breakfast (from 8), lunch and tea till 4:30.
PRICE RANGE: $$
You'll be charmed as all get out when you enter this tea room in an old house dating back to 1740. Besides the tea, they also serve big breakfast and lunch menus with items costing sometimes less than you'd pay at a McDonald's. Great eggs Benedict, pecan smokehouse bacon, lemon poppy seed hotcakes, baked stuffed

French toast. Wide variety of lovely sandwiches for lunch. Pies, cakes and pastries for tea.

**EARTHLY DELIGHTS**
15 W Bay Rd, Osterville, 508-420-2206
https://earthlydelightscapecod.wordpress.com/
CUISINE: Vegan
DRINKS: No Booze
SERVING: Breakfast/Lunch
PRICE RANGE: $
NEIGHBORHOOD: Osterville
Vegetarian and vegan cuisine, eco-mind sandwiches, breakfast plates, smoothies, and juices. Great freshly baked muffins every morning.

**EMBARGO**
453 Main St, Hyannis Port, 508-771-9700
www.embargorestaurant.com
CUISINE: Tapas/Sushi
DRINKS: Full Bar
SERVING: Lunch, Dinner
PRICE RANGE: $$

This popular eatery is a favorite with the hipster crowd. For our purposes here, that will include me! Here you'll find tapas, pizza and a lot more. The hot tapas menu runs to over 2 dozen items, from scallops wrapped in bacon to mussels a la blanca to hickory smoked baby back ribs. Big juicy steaks are also offered, including a 24-oz cowboy rib eye, along with crispy flatbreads. Favorites include Kobe Beef sliders (half price on Tuesday). Oh, and from 4:30 to 6, they have a happy hour with half-priced oysters and tapas. There's also live music in a modern lounge setting and live jazz at dinner till 9:30.

**EMBER PIZZA**
600 Massachusetts 28, Harwich Port, 508-430-0407
www.emberpizza.com
CUISINE: Pizza

DRINKS: Full Bar
SERVING: Dinner; closed Mon
PRICE RANGE: $$$
This popular pizzeria offers a menu of coal-fired, thin-crust pizza, wings and pasta.
You must try the Spinach and artichoke dip and the Gorgonzola garlic bread. Specials include the Chicken bacon ranch pizza. This is a pizza lovers' destination.

**FANCY'S**
699 Main St, Osterville, 508-428-6954
www.fancysmarket.com
CUISINE: Deli/Market
DRINKS: Beer & Wine
SERVING: 7 a.m. – 7 p.m.
PRICE RANGE: $$
NEIGHBORHOOD: Osterville
If you want to get some great take-out, come to this local market that offers a nice selection of freshly made subs, wraps and paninis, but they also have some great prepared foods, like pork tenderloin with roasted veggies, deep dish lasagna, baked salmon with a saffron cream sauce, things like that. There's also a good reasonably priced wine selection and lots of gourmet items for sale..

**FANIZZI'S BY THE SEA**
539 Commercial St, Provincetown 508-487-1964
www.fanizzisrestaurant.com
CUISINE: American/Seafood
DRINKS: Full Bar
SERVING: Lunch, Dinner

PRICE RANGE: $$
CUISINE: American / Seafood / Italian
DRINKS: Full Bar
SERVING: Lunch, Dinner
PRICE RANGE: $$
This locals' favorite offers and a menu of Italian classics and American seafood. Lots of towns have a restaurant like this, that started off serving classic Italian cuisine that later morphed into a combination of Italian and America. We used to call that assimilation, but that's a dirty word these days. Anyway, this is what Fanizzi might be called. So, you'll have your Chicken Piccata and your Eggplant Parmigiana in a homemade marinara sauce, but you'll also find Braised Short Ribs and a Baked Cod with a mustard nut crust. But hey, whatever they serve here, it's damned good, I will say that. It's also right on the water, so you have spectacular views of Provincetown harbor. They even suggest you come here when the weather is at its worst. And they're right. I was in P-town one winter weekend on business and a n'or-easter hit the Cape. We came here for an early dinner, and it was thrilling to watch the waves crash up against the windows. Open 7 days a week year-round for lunch and dinner.

**FAR LAND PROVISIONS**
150 Bradford St, Provincetown, 508-487-0045
www.farlandprovisions.com
CUISINE: Deli/Bakery
DRINKS: No Booze
SERVING: 7 a.m. – 6 p.m.
PRICE RANGE: $

NEIGHBORHOOD: P-town
All-day deli/bakery with a nice selection of sandwiches, light fare like mac & cheese, meatloaf, and cinnamon rolls. Extensive deli section. They champion a "pier to plate" program, by which I mean they serve as much fish caught by local fishermen as they can. Their market sells beer, wine, spirits, and organic eggs.

**FIN**
800 Main St, Dennis, 508-385-2096
www.fincapecod.com
CUISINE: Seafood
DRINKS: Full Bar
SERVING: Dinner; closed Sun & Mon
PRICE RANGE: $$$
Located in an antique home, this high-end restaurant offers a menu of contemporary seafood. Creative wine selection offers something for everyone. Delicious desserts. Reservations recommended.

**FISHERMAN'S VIEW**
20 Freezer Rd, Sandwich, 508-591-0088
www.fishermensview.com
CUISINE: Seafood
DRINKS: Full bar
SERVING: Lunch & Dinner
PRICE RANGE: $$
Locals' favorite with a classic Cape Cod seafood menu. Picks. Swordfish Steak and Striped Bass. Lobster roll is worth getting. Lots of seating. Nice cocktail menu.

**FIVE BAYS BISTRO**

825 Main St, Osterville, 508-420-5559
www.fivebaysbistro.com
CUISINE: New American
DRINKS: Full Bar
SERVING: Dinner; open Sat & Sun
PRICE RANGE: $$$

Owners Jamie Surprenant and Tim Sourza offer a sophisticated menu of creative American cuisine. Menu favorites include: Honey-Soy Glazed Salmon and Braised Pork Shank. Creative wine list.

**FRONT STREET**

230 Commercial St, Provincetown, 508-487-9715
www.frontstreetrestaurant.com
CUISINE: Italian
DRINKS: Full Bar
SERVING: Dinner
PRICE RANGE: $$$

Kathy & Donna are the owners here in this lovely eatery situated on the ground floor of a Victorian mansion. Italy and southern France are the culinary inspirations behind the food here. Amarone roasted boneless beef short rib, truffled Sachetti alla Carbonara, eggplant Involtini, Italian sausage with polenta, lots of great pasta creations.

**GERARDI'S CAFÉ**

902 Massachusetts 28, South Yarmouth, 508-394-3111
www.gerardiscafe.com
CUISINE: Italian/Gluten-free
DRINKS: Full Bar

SERVING: Dinner
PRICE RANGE: $$
This popular eatery offers a menu of classic Sicilian-style cuisine with gluten-free options. This place offers a nice dining experience for the entire family but it's romantic enough for a date night. Menu favorites include: Veal piccata and Blue crab fettuccini. The bar serves a variety of traditional Italian cocktails.

**GINA'S BY THE SEA**
134 Taunton Ave, Dennis, 508-385-3213
www.ginasbythesea.com
CUISINE: Italian
DRINKS: Full Bar
SERVING: Dinner; closed Mon - Wed
PRICE RANGE: $$$
This place has become a Cape Cod institution with a menu of Italian-American classics. Menu picks include: Shrimp Scampi and Eggplant Parmesan. Operating over sixty years, this place still attracts a bog loyal crowd, so reservations are recommended.

**GLASS ONION**
37 N Main St, Falmouth, 508-540-3730
www.theglassoniondining.com
CUISINE: American
DRINKS: Full Bar
SERVING: Dinner; closed Sun - Mon
PRICE RANGE: $$$
This elegant restaurant offers a menu of New American cuisine. Popular choices include: Lobster strudel appetizer and Shrimp & mussels. Global wines and creative cocktails like their popular watermelon mojito. No reservations.

**GRUMPY'S**
1408 Massachusetts 6A, East Dennis, 508-385-2911
www.grumpyscapecod.com
CUISINE: American/Diner
DRINKS: No Booze
SERVING: Breakfast, Lunch, & Dinner

PRICE RANGE: $$
Not an elegant eatery at all, just a family-owned roadside stop serving great all-American comfort food. Great breakfasts. Favorites include: Homemade corned beef hash. Try their homemade muffins (8-10 varieties). Open all year.
live Irish music (on the weekends). Menu picks include: the Belfast burger made with pulled pork and bacon.

**HARVEST GALLERY WINE BAR**
776 Main St, Dennis, 508-385-2444
www.harvestgallerywinebar.com
CUISINE: American
DRINKS: Beer & wine only
SERVING: Wednesday-Sundays from 4:30, when happy hour begins
PRICE RANGE: $$

The intimate, diverse gallery features more than 30 artists and their works - paintings, collages, sculptures, assemblages, textiles, photography, glass, jewelry and, of course, the culinary arts and even entertainment. Pickled local eggs; Thai crab lettuce wraps; a lovely Panini of mozzarella, roasted tomatoes, basil pesto, avocado on crusty bread; French dip (which you don't see that often anymore, and this one is good); a nice turkey melt. Good place to eat at the bar if you're alone because the staff is so friendly.

**IMPUDENT OYSTER**
15 Chatham Bars Ave, Chatham, 508-945-3545
www.theimpudentoyster.com
CUISINE: Seafood
DRINKS: Full Bar
SERVING: Lunch and dinner
PRICE RANGE: $$$
Set in a beautiful old house, you'll find this a romantic place for dinner. Portions are big and the

food is excellent: Sea scallops wrapped in bacon with onions, garlic and parsley; oysters Rockefeller; Vermont butternut bisque; mussels in wine; butternut ravioli; lobster croquettes; blueberry pie. The lobster roll for lunch is a treat.

**INAHO**

157 Rte 6A, Yarmouth Port, 508-362-5522
www.inaho-sushi.com
CUISINE: Japanese; Sushi
DRINKS: Full Bar
SERVING: Mon-Sat 4:30 pm - 10 pm
PRICE RANGE: $$$
Serves a full range of sushi as well as some hot and cold Japanese favorites like yaki gyoza (pan-fried shrimp served with vegetable dumplings) and panko scallop (kabobs of fried breaded scallops).

**JT'S SEAFOOD**

2689 Main St, Brewster, 508-896-3355
www.jt-seafood.com
CUISINE: Seafood
DRINKS: Beer & Wine Only
SERVING: Lunch, Dinner
PRICE RANGE: $$
This old-style New England seafood shack serves food from its counter and guests can eat inside or on the outdoor patio. Menu picks include: the Grilled Salmon and the very spectacular Cheeseburgers. For dessert they offer soft serve ice cream.

**THE JERK CAFÉ**
1319 Massachusetts 28, South Yarmouth, 508-394-1944
www.thejerkcafe.com
CUISINE: Caribbean
DRINKS: No Booze
SERVING: Lunch, Dinner
PRICE RANGE: $
This popular café offers a menu of Jamaican Jerk Style Caribbean cuisine. Limited seating. They're known for their great BBQ sauce and Jerk Chicken.

**JIMMY'S HIDEAWAY**
179 Commercial St, Provincetown, 508-487-1011
www.jimmyshideaway.com
CUISINE: American (New), Diners
DRINKS: Full Bar
SERVING: Dinner nightly from 5:30.
PRICE RANGE: $$$
NEIGHBORHOOD: Provincetown
It’s hard to miss the door and trim which is painted in a bright red as you walk down a few old brick steps to a slightly subterranean and slightly romantic eatery with a dark pub-like ambience with rich wood paneling and low lighting. I love this place off season when it’s snowing outside. That must be because they have very comfortable chairs at the bar, so this makes a great place to plant your butt for the evening, have a few drinks and then dinner. When the weather’s all right, you can sit outside. Menu (changes with the seasons) features American fare with a European twist. Favorites: BBQ Spare Ribs; a very good Wedge salad with one of the best blue cheese dressings I’ve had lately; Grilled oysters with jalapeno-lemon butter; Scallops Piccata. Reservations recommended.

**JOON BAR + KITCHEN**
133 Commercial St, Provincetown, 508-413-9336
www.joonbar.com
CUISINE: Wine Bar/American (New)
DRINKS: Full Bar
SERVING: Lunch, Dinner, Brunch
PRICE RANGE: $$$

NEIGHBORHOOD: Provincetown
In a little white cottage, you'll find this popular modern and yet quaint eatery in a longish room with a comfortable bar (good chairs) on one side, with a few high-tops separating the bar from a long banquette against the wall. Featuring seasonal New American cuisine, with emphasis on "seasonal." Favorites: Duck Sliders on a buttermilk biscuit; Char-grilled NY Strip; Bouillabaisse made with lobster, mussels, shrimp, clams, halibut in a saffron tomato stew. Nice wine list and creative cocktails like the Joon Margarita (Tequila plata, Ancho Reyes, agave nectar, lime).

**KAROO KAFE**
3 Main St -Ste 32B, Eastham, 508-255-8288
www.karoorestaurants.com
CUISINE: Vegetarian/African
DRINKS: Beer & Wine Only
SERVING: Lunch, Dinner
PRICE RANGE: $$
This casual eatery offers counter service. Menu features African inspired cuisine with variety of vegetarian and gluten-free options. Menu picks include: Ostrich burger and Chakalaka salad.

**KKATIES'S BURGER BAR**
334 Main St, Hyannis, 508-771-4282
www.kkaties.com
CUISINE: Burgers
DRINKS: Full bar
SERVING: Lunch & Dinner
PRICE RANGE: $$

NEIGHBORHOOD: Hyannis
Looking like a typical pub, this place is known for its burgers and they offer a variety of burgers and sandwiches. Creative cocktails.

**KREAM & KONE**
961 Main St, West Dennis, 508-394-0808
www.kreamnkone.com
CUISINE: Seafood
DRINKS: Beer & Wine Only
SERVING: Lunch, Dinner
PRICE RANGE: $$
Known for their fried seafood, this counter-service eatery offers casual dining by the river with a menu of seafood treats, fried clams, and sandwiches. For dessert try one of the 27 soft serve flavors.

**L'ALOUETTE BISTRO**
787 Massachusetts 28, Harwich Port, 508-430-0405
www.frenchbistrocapecod.com
CUISINE: French
DRINKS: Full Bar
SERVING: Dinner; closed Tues & Wed
PRICE RANGE: $$$
Located in a quaint building with dormer windows on the second floor, this casual bistro offers a menu of global cuisine, but the emphasis is on classic French cooking—that's the star at this polished, low-key place. For a starter, get the little Beignets, really just crab, corn and scallion fritters. They're delicious. Menu favorites include: the Calves liver, which you don't see very often. Here they do it right with the caramelized onions, smoked bacon, madeira sauce,

mashed potatoes. My other favorite is the Duck Two Ways, by which they mean you get the grilled duck breast as well as the leg confit with a raspberry sauce. There are lots of other good dishes on this lovely menu.

**LA TACODILLA**
702 Ma 28, West Dennis, 508-292-8817
www.cleanslateeatery.com
CUISINE: Vegetarian/American (Traditional)
DRINKS: Beer & Wine
SERVING: Breakfast/Lunch/Dinner; closed Sun & Mon
PRICE RANGE: $$$$
NEIGHBORHOOD: West Dennis
Locals' favorite that serves healthy dishes that are served to you by the chefs. Favorites: Day Boat Scallop and Flank Steak. Nice wine pairings. Menu changes weekly.

**LAMBERT'S RAINBOW FRUIT**
1000 W Main St, Centerville, 508-477-0655
www.lambertsfarmmarket.com
CUISINE: Fruits & Veggies
DRINKS: Beer & Wine
SERVING: Breakfast/Lunch/Dinner
PRICE RANGE: $$$
NEIGHBORHOOD: Centerville
This place offers made-to-order giant deli sandwiches, a salad and soup bar, deli, and a great selection of fresh fruit, herbs, and veggies. Tasty baked goods and desserts. Closes around 7 p.m.

**LAND HO!**
Route 6A at Cove Rd, Orleans, 508-255-5165
www.land-ho.com
CUISINE: American
DRINKS: Full Bar
SERVING: Lunch, Dinner
PRICE RANGE: $$
Very popular eatery during season, so try to come at off-peak hours to avoid the crowds. Known for their crazy décor and big baskets of chicken and fries. Menu is mostly American comfort food but there's also seafood. Menu picks include: Grilled chicken club and Crab cakes.

**LANDFALL**
9 Luscombe Ave., Woods Hole, 508-548-1758
www.landfallwoodshole.com

CUISINE: Seafood
DRINKS: Full Bar
SERVING: Lunch and dinner, but hours vary. Call ahead. Open April–November.
PRICE RANGE: $$
Everything used to build this place (it opened in 1946) came from "somewhere else." Every board, plant, piece of stained glass or window has its own story, and they'll be happy to tell it to you. Some of the wood came from shipwrecks, some from old houses that fell down where the wood was recycled here. The harpoons, buoys, oars and netting were gifts from friends. Baked stuffed lobster and the lobster Savannah (with sherry and cream) are good. The fried scallops melt in your mouth.

**THE LANES BOWL & BISTRO**
9 Green St, Mashpee Commons 774-228-2291

www.lanesbowlandbistro.com
CUISINE: American
DRINKS: Full Bar
SERVING: Lunch, Dinner
PRICE RANGE: $$
This hip bowling alley offers a casual bistro with a menu of American classics, flatbread sandwiches, and hearty pizzas. Favorites include: Fried asparagus and Chicken Broccoli Alfredo pizza. Live music and an outdoor café.

**LIAM MAGUIRE'S IRISH PUB AND RESTAURANT**
273 Main St, Falmouth, 508-548-0285
www.liammaguire.com /
CUISINE: Irish
DRINKS: Full Bar
SERVING: Lunch, Dinner
PRICE RANGE: $$
A pub and restaurant serving classic Irish fare. Nice wine list and selection of draft beer. Known for the great burgers and huge lobster rolls. Live entertainment.

**LAURA & TONY'S KITCHEN**
5960 Route 6, Eastham, 508-240-6096
www.lauraandtonyskitchen.com
CUISINE: New American; Breakfast; Brunch
DRINKS: Full Bar
SERVING: Sat 7:30-noon; Sun 7:30-1 pm
PRICE RANGE: $$
Nothing simpler than this place that packs 'em in with an all-you-can-eat breakfast buffet. All the baking is

done on-premise, so their excellent gooey cinnamon rolls are made fresh just before you eat them. They claim everything is so fresh they don't even have a can opener in the kitchen.

**LOBSTER POT**
321 Commercial St, Provincetown, 508-487-0842
www.ptownlobsterpot.com
CUISINE: Seafood
DRINKS: Full Bar
SERVING: Lunch and Dinner
PRICE RANGE: $$
Nice selection of raw bar items: oysters with sour cream and caviar; crab claw cocktail, lobster avocado cocktail, oysters and clams on the half shell. Main courses hit all the right hunger spots with baked Portuguese clams, Asian steamed littlenecks, lobster

ravioli, blackened tuna sashimi, sautéed squid. Sit in the unpretentious room and look out over the harbor. Spacious bar, outdoor deck.

**LOCAL BREAK**
4550 State Hwy, Eastham, 508-255-6100
www.local-break.com
CUISINE: American
DRINKS: Full Bar
SERVING: Dinner
PRICE RANGE: $$
Busy eatery that offers a creative menu of American cuisine. Known for their house burger and hot wings served with buffalo bleu cheese sauce. Menu of creative cocktails like the candied cranberry margarita.

**THE LOCAL JUICE BAR + PANTRY**
539 South St., Hyannis, 508-827-7447
www.thelocaljuice.com
CUISINE: Juices/Smoothies
DRINKS: No Booze
SERVING: Breakfast/Lunch
PRICE RANGE: $$
NEIGHBORHOOD: Hyannis
Mainly a juice and smoothie place but they also offer a variety of snacks, fresh eggs, honey, hot sauce, chocolate, and produce.

**MAC'S SEAFOOD**
macsseafood.com
Mac's has several old-style seafood shacks but has branched out to offer white-tablecloth service in some

of his locations. Check to see which ones are close to you, as well as what kind of lunch or dining experience you're looking for. They have it all, as well as half a dozen fish markets if you want to buy your seafood and cook it at home. Me? I prefer to let Mac's more than professional team do the shucking, do the sauteeing, do the grilling, do the broiling and do the baking. Not to mention the cleaning up. These are all good for your basic Cape Cod seafood bingeing.

**MAC'S MARKET & KITCHEN**
4680 RTE 6, Eastham, 508-255-6900
**MAC'S FISH & LOBSTER**
Cornfield Marketplace
1291 Main St, Rte 28, Chatham, 508-945-1173
**MAC'S FISHHOUSE**
85 Shank Painter Rd, P'town, 508-487-6227

**MAC'S ON THE PIER**
265 Commercial Street, Wellfleet, 508-349-9611
**MAC'S SHACK**
91 Commercial St, Wellfleet, 508-349-6333

**MAD MINNOW**
554 Main St Rt 28, Harwich Port, 774-209-3977
www.madminnow.com
CUISINE: Gastropub/American (New)
DRINKS: Full bar
SERVING: Dinner – Lunch on weekends
PRICE RANGE: $$
NEIGHBORHOOD: Harwich Port
Hangout for young hipsters serving delicious food. Favorites: Crab cakes and Tuna cannoli. Other treats include the scallop roll and gnocchi. Casual dining inside and outside on picnic tables.

**MARSHLAND RESTAURANT**
109 Rte 6A. Sandwich, 508-888-9824
www.marshlandrestaurant.com
CUISINE: American
DRINKS: Full Bar
SERVING: Breakfast, Lunch & Dinner; open daily
PRICE RANGE: $$
This place has been a landmark for over 50 years and open 7 days a week. The classic American menu features breakfast, lunch, and dinner. A bakery section offers muffins, pies, cakes, and cookies.

**MARSHSIDE**
28 Bridge St, E Dennis, 508-385-4010
www.themarshside.com

CUISINE: Seafood
DRINKS: Full Bar
SERVING: Lunch, Dinner
PRICE RANGE: $$
This casual eatery offers a creative menu of American cuisine and seafood. Sit by the windows and enjoy a great view of the marsh. Favorites include: Cobb salad and the fresh oysters. Great bar.

**MATTAKEESE WHARF**
273 Millway, Barnstable Harbor, 508-362-4511
www.mattakeese.com
CUISINE: Seafood
DRINKS: Full Bar
SERVING: Lunch, Dinner, & Sunday Brunch
PRICE RANGE: $$$
This place suckers people in with its great location, right on the dock. People pull up, tie off and run up to

eat and drink here. Stick to the drinks and if you're really hungry, go for the raw bar items. They're consistently good. If you want a more substantial meal, eat elsewhere.

**MEWS**
429 Commercial St, Provincetown, 508-487-1500
https://mewsptown.com/
CUISINE: American
DRINKS: Full Bar
SERVING: Dinner
PRICE RANGE: $$$
This popular eatery offers two levels and great views of the water. Menu favorites include: Lobster Risotto and Scallops. Nice wine list and huge vodka collection.

**MISAKI**
379 Main St, Hyannis, 508-771-3771
www.misakisushi.com
CUISINE: Japanese
DRINKS: Full Bar
SERVING: Dinner; closed Sun & Mon
PRICE RANGE: $$
This little Japanese eatery offers a menu of traditional sushi and creative rolls. Try their signature Cape Cod roll. Favorites in addition to sushi include: Chicken Teriyaki Grilled chicken and Vegetable Tempura. Reservations recommended.

**MOM & POPS BURGERS**
1603 Main St, Chatham, 774-840-4144
www.momandpopschatham.com

CUISINE: Burgers/Flipino
DRINKS: Beer & Wine
SERVING: Lunch & Dinner
PRICE RANGE: $$
NEIGHBORHOOD: Chatham
Great casual spot serving burgers, hot dogs, lumpia, frappes, craft beer and wine. Favorites: Fried chicken sandwich and the California burger. Gluten-free options.

**MONTANO'S RESTAURANT**
481 U.S. 6, North Truro, 508-487-2026
www.montanos.com
CUISINE: Italian
DRINKS: Full Bar
SERVING: Dinner
PRICE RANGE: $$
Cute little family-style eatery that offers a varied menu of New England fare and Italian cuisine. Favorites include: Chicken Parmigiana and Fettuccine Alfredo. Tasty homemade sangria

**MOONCUSSERS TAVERN**
86 Sisson Rd, Harwich Port, 508-430-1230
www.mooncusserstavern.com
CUISINE: Tapas
DRINKS: Full Bar
SERVING: Dinner
PRICE RANGE: $$$
This popular tavern is known for its tapas but also serves a variety of appetizers and entrees. Favorites include: Pan Seared Duck Breast and California Tuna

Avo Burger. Extensive wine list and great selection of martinis.

**NAKED OYSTER**
410 Main St, Hyannis, 508-778-6500
www.nakedoyster.com
CUISINE: New American, Seafood
DRINKS: Full Bar
SERVING: Lunch & dinner daily
PRICE RANGE: $$$
One of the best raw bars on the Cape. Lobster bisque is very good here. Oyster stew as well, with sherry, cream and shallots. Pistachio crusted Scottish salmon

is a winner. Blackened haddock, sautéed jumbo Thai shrimp.

**NAPI'S**
7 Freeman St, Provincetown, 508-487-1145
www.napisptown.com
CUISINE: Seafood
DRINKS: Full Bar
SERVING: Dinner
PRICE RANGE: $$
This unique eatery offers an international, seafood-focused menu. Menu picks include: Chicken Picatta and Tenderloin with Brie. Vegetarian options available. Eclectic atmosphere in a venue filled with art.

**OCEAN HOUSE RESTAURANT**
425 Old Wharf Rd, Dennisport, 508-394-0700
www.oceanhouserestaurant.com
CUISINE: New American
DRINKS: Full Bar
SERVING: Wed-Sun 4-11(lounge opens at 4; dinner from 5)
PRICE RANGE: $$$
Very nice romantic spot. Perfect for Date Night. Sliders with "truffled ketchup" and crispy onions; orange glazed BBQ ribs; seafood bruschetta (mussels, clams, shrimp, lobster, white wine and tomato, garlic) over Tuscan bread; lump crab cake. Go a little early to get a table by the window overlooking the water.

**OLD YARMOUTH INN**
223 Route 6A, Yarmouth Port, 508-362-9962
www.oldyarmouthinn.com
CUISINE: American
DRINKS: Full Bar
SERVING: Lunch, Dinner
PRICE RANGE: $$$

The Inn has been an institution in Cape Cod and is known for serving the best fresh fish, shellfish, steak and pasta. Menu picks include: Chef's Vegetable Risotto and Roast Maple Leaf Farm Half Duck. Great choice for Sunday brunch. Award winning wine selection.

**ORGANIC MARKET**
640 Main St, Dennis Port, 508-760-3043
www.omorganicmarket.com
CUISINE: Juice Bar/Health Market
DRINKS: No Booze
SERVING: Breakfast/Lunch/Early Dinner
PRICE RANGE: $$$
NEIGHBORHOOD: Dennis Port
Health market with a juice bar. Favorites: Chicken salad sandwich and the avocado toast with red pepper flakes. Top-notch selection of products, organic vegetables, nuts, seeds and grains.

**ORLEANS INN**
3 Old Country Rd, Orleans, 508-255-2222
www.orleansinn.com
CUISINE: American
DRINKS: Full Bar
SERVING: Breakfast, Lunch, Dinner
PRICE RANGE: $$
A well-known hotel and restaurant filled with history dating back to 1875. A charming place for a waterfront dining offering a menu of classic Cape Cod cuisine. Menu favorites include: Blackened Salmon with a Cajun Remoulade and Chicken Picatta. Nice selection of desserts on the chef's table.

**OSTERIA LA CIVETTA**
133 Main St, Falmouth, 508-540-1616
www.osterialacivetta.com
CUISINE: Italian
DRINKS: Full Bar
SERVING: Lunch, Dinner
PRICE RANGE: $$
This Italian eatery offers a menu of classic housemade pastas and great Italian wine list with pretty reasonable prices. Favorites specials include: Saltimbocca alla Romana and Crema di Funghi. Try the tiramisu for dessert. It's hard to beat and made fresh daily.

**OYSTER COMPANY**
202 Depot St, Dennisport, 508-398-4600
www.theoystercompany.com
CUISINE: Seafood

DRINKS: Full Bar
SERVING: Lunch on Fri, Sat & Sun, Dinner nightly
PRICE RANGE: $$$
This locals' favorite also attracts the tourists who enjoy the diverse seafood menu. Favorite picks include: Oysters Rockefeller and Honey Dijon-Glazed Salmon. Also great steaks and wine list. Known for their house martinis. Reservations recommended.

**PAIN D'AVIGNON**
15 Hinckley Rd, Hyannis, 508-778-8588
www.paindavignon.com
CUISINE: French /Bakery
DRINKS: Full Bar
SERVING: Breakfast, Lunch, & Dinner
PRICE RANGE: $$
This European-style bakery offers a menu of French bistro fare as well as an assortment of breads and pastries. Picks include: Tartare of Beef and Grilled Spanish Octopus. You must try their sweets like the berry panna cotta and the chocolate croissant.

**PALIO PIZZERIA**
435 Main St, Hyannis, 508-771-7004
www.paliopizzeria.com
CUISINE: Pizza
DRINKS: Beer & Wine
SERVING: Lunch, Dinner
PRICE RANGE: $$
This casual pizzeria is known for its brick-oven pies but also serves delicious Italian fare like pastas and cannoli. Live music.

**PATE'S**
1260 Main St, Chatham, 508-945-9777
www.patesrestaurant.com
CUISINE: Seafood
DRINKS: Full Bar
SERVING: Lunch, Dinner
PRICE RANGE: $$$
Known for their great choice of seafood but this place is also a favorite of steak lovers. Favorites include: Baked Chatham Haddock and Filet Mignon en Brochette. Huge wine list and a separate lounge.

**PB BOULANGERIE**
15 Lecount Hollow Rd, Wellfleet, 508-349-1600
www.pbboulangeriebistro.com
CUISINE: French/Bakery
DRINKS: Full Bar

SERVING: Dinner on Fri & Sat, Brunch on Sun, closed Mon - Thurs
PRICE RANGE: $$
This unique spot is half bakery and half bistro. A great choice for either French fare or classic pastries. Entrée picks include: Half-Cooked Smoked Salmon and Long Island Duck Breast a l'Orange.

**PEARL**
250 Commercial St, Wellfleet, 508-349-2999
www.wellfleetpearl.com
CUISINE: American/Seafood
DRINKS: Full Bar
SERVING: Lunch, Dinner
PRICE RANGE: $$
This family-friendly eatery offers a classic menu of New England standards, salads, steaks, and a raw bar. Picks include: Teriyaki hibachi steak and Baked cod. Busy during the summer months. Great view when dining on the deck.

**PECORINO ROMANO**
605 Main St Rt 6A, Dennis, 508-694-6333
www.pecorinoromanotuscancuisine.com
CUISINE: Italian
DRINKS: Full bar
SERVING: Dinner
PRICE RANGE: $$
NEIGHBORHOOD: Dennis
Extremely popular eatery serving authentic Italian cuisine with a Tuscan flare. (I think the popularity of this place has to do with its reasonable prices as much as the so-so-quality of its food.) Menu picks:

Eggplant rollantini and Veal Parmigiana. Nice selection of wines and desserts. Full menu or prix–fixe option.

**PISCES**
2653 Main St, Chatham, 508-432-4600
www.piscesofchatham.com
CUISINE: American
DRINKS: Full Bar
SERVING: Lunch, Dinner
PRICE RANGE: $$$
Local in a charming old house, this casual eatery offers a menu of standard American fare and Mediterranean-inspired seafood. Menu favorites include: Maine Lobster Ravioli and Yellowtail Tuna. Impressive wine list. Everything is made fresh here including the delicious desserts.

**PICKLE JAR KITCHEN**
170 Main St, Falmouth, 508-540-6760
www.picklejarkitchen.com
CUISINE: American
DRINKS: Full Bar
SERVING: Breakfast & Lunch; closed Tues
PRICE RANGE: $$
Popular café serving classic American comfort food. Good lunch and brunch spot with a variety of menus. Favorites include: Pastrami seasoned smoked salmon with bagel and Blueberry muffin French toast.

**POST OFFICE CAFÉ & CABARET**
303 Commercial St, Provincetown, 508-487-3892
www.postofficecafe.net/

CUISINE: American (Traditional)
DRINKS: Full Bar
SERVING: Breakfast, Lunch, Dinner
PRICE RANGE: $$
NEIGHBORHOOD: Provincetown
Two-level café offering American fare on the first floor and upstairs a cabaret offering acts like RuPaul Drag Race winner Raja and The All-Male Dance Revue. Menu picks: Omelets for breakfast; Chicken quesadilla, Lobster roll and Sirloin burger for lunch; Portuguese Kale Soup, Shrimp & Grits, Homemade Meatloaf, Bone-in rib eye for dinner. A few tables under umbrellas outside in good weather. Great cocktails.

**THE RED COTTAGE**
36 Old Bass River Rd, South Dennis, 508-394-2923
www.redcottagerestaurant.com
CUISINE: American (Traditional) / Sandwiches

DRINKS: No Booze
SERVING: Breakfast & Lunch
PRICE RANGE: $$ **<u>Cash only</u>**
NEIGHBORHOOD: South Dennis
Diner-style eatery offering traditional American fare specializing in breakfast, which is why it's so popular in the morning, with superior pancakes and homemade corned beef hash. In Miami, where I'm from, I often eat at Joe's Stone Crab early in the morning—because though they're known for stone crabs, what's not known is they serve a kick-ass breakfast (that's also very cheap). I go because the quality is so good. The same for this place—their bacon is cut thick—9 slices to the pound, and comes in Applewood, Black Pepper or Cajun flavors. The eggs and everything else is of the highest quality. Oh, and though their regular home fries are plenty good enough, specify that you want their "Red Cottage Home Fries," a little cut above—these mix the usual grilled potatoes with lots more: onions, tomatoes, ham, green peppers & mushrooms combined with special spices and topped with lemon Hollandaise sauce. (In fact, this side dish is a meal in itself.) Cash only.

**THE RED INN**
15 Commercial St, Provincetown, 508-487-7334
www.theredinn.com
CUISINE: New American
DRINKS: Full bar; happy hour from 2:30 to 5; raw bar specials
SERVING: Lunch and dinner
PRICE RANGE: $$

This inn (from 1915) has a great restaurant: pan roasted local cod on a bed of rosemary potatoes and applewood bacon. The lamb chops are tops as well. The bar here makes a great place to grab a drink and absorb the atmosphere, or even better, enjoy the sunset.

**RED NUN BAR & GRILL**
746 Main St, Chatham, 508-348-0469
673 Main St, Dennis Port, 508-394-BUOY (2869)
www.rednun.com
CUISINE: American
DRINKS: Full bar
SERVING: Lunch and dinner daily from 11:30, except Sunday, when it's closed
PRICE RANGE: $$
Situated in a lovely red clapboard house with indoor and outdoor seating is this fun place. Serves up fried lobster; stuffed Quahogs; beer battered onion rings; fish tacos; fried or baked scallops; 6 or 7 burger creations (including the option to "build your own"); pulled pork sandwiches. (Their location in Dennis Port is in a simple brick building, but the food and vibe make up for the lackluster setting.)

**RED PHEASANT INN**
905 Main St (Rte 6A), Dennis, 508-385-2133
www.redpheasantinn.com
CUISINE: New American
DRINKS: Full bar
SERVING: Tues-Sun, dinner only from 5
PRICE RANGE: $$

A converted 200-year-old barn is the setting for this rustic charmer serving up exciting creative dishes: the chowder here has cherrystones and scallops with thyme; white bean crostini; there's a nightly game special, like venison or elk; roasted rack of lamb with gratin potatoes & panna cotta.

**RED'S AT SEA CREST BEACH HOTEL**
350 Quaker Rd, North Falmouth, 508-356-2136
www.seacrestbeachhotel.com
CUISINE: American
DRINKS: Full Bar
SERVING: Lunch, Dinner
PRICE RANGE: $$
Located in Sea Crest Beach Hotel, this favorite seafood spot also serves classic American fare. Great ocean view with poolside & porch dining. Great Lobster, BBQ and pizza.

**RELISH**
93 Commercial St, Provincetown, 508-487-8077
www.ptownrelish.com/
CUISINE: Bakery; deli
DRINKS: No booze
SERVING: Breakfast and lunch (till 3 weekdays, till 5 weekends).
PRICE RANGE: $$
Dozens of baked goods: double fudge brownies, chocolate dipped macaroons, triple chip cookies, cupcakes, pies, you name it. They also have an excellent selection of delicious sandwiches for lunch. Director John Waters loves this place.

**ROSS' GRILL**
237 Commercial St, Provincetown, 508-487-8878
www.rossgrillptown.com
CUISINE: American
DRINKS: Full Bar
SERVING: Lunch, Dinner; closed Mon - Wed
PRICE RANGE: $$$
Located on the harbor front, this casual grill offers a menu of New American cuisine.
Menu favorites include: Cape Cod Seafood Stew and Fresh Vegan Ravioli with Marinara Sauce.
Impressive wine list with over 75 wines served by the glass. Tapas & Raw Bar Happy Hour. Reservations recommended.

**RUGGIE'S BREAKFAST & LUNCH**
707 Main St, Harwich, 508-432-0625
www.ruggiescapecod.com

CUISINE: Breakfast/Sandwiches
DRINKS: No Booze
SERVING: Breakfast & Lunch
PRICE RANGE: $$
Located in historic Harwich, this little café is a nice choice for breakfast or a quick lunch. Menu favorites include: Chicken & Waffles and Breakfast Nachos with eggs.
Open year round.

**SAGAMORE INN**
1131 MA-6A, Sagamore, 508-888-9707
www.sagamoreinncapecod.com
CUISINE: American (New)
DRINKS: Full Bar
SERVING: Lunch & Dinner; Breakfast on weekends
PRICE RANGE: $$
New owners, Michael and Suzanne Bilodeau, celebrate the old owners by serving all the old favorites. Classic roadhouse atmosphere with a great menu of comfort food – mostly Italian and seafood. Creative desserts.

**SAM DIEGO'S**
950 Iyannough Rd, Hyannis, 508-771-8816
www.samdiegos.com
CUISINE: Mexican
DRINKS: Full Bar
SERVING: Lunch, Dinner
PRICE RANGE: $$
This Americanized Mexican eatery offers a full menu of award-winning Mexican and Tex-Mex selections. Patio dining in warm months.

**SESUIT HARBOR CAFÉ**
357 Sesuit Neck Rd, Dennis, 508-385-6134
https://sesuit-harbor-cafe.com/
CUISINE: Seafood
DRINKS: No booze, but you can BYOB
SERVING: Breakfast (from 7am), lunch and early dinner daily till dusk.
PRICE RANGE: $$ / **cash only**
A real seafood shack that's a locals' hangout. (They come for the lobster roll—there's none better. Comes with fries and slaw. It is worth a drive.) The plate of scallops is very good. A half-order is more than sufficient. The place is tucked away in a marina here on the north shore. You order inside, take a number, go out and sit at a picnic table till they bring your food to you. If you opt for breakfast, go for the lobster omelette. Quite a full menu. Nothing fancy. Lots of boat traffic. Repeat: cash only.

**SIENA**
17 Steeple St, Mashpee, 508-477-5929
www.siena.us
CUISINE: Italian/Pizza
DRINKS: Full Bar
SERVING: Lunch, Dinner
PRICE RANGE: $$
A locals' favorite that welcomes tourists during season. Menu features Roman-style pizzas and hearty Italian fare. Great handpicked wine list. Good selection of gluten-free options.

## SIMPLY DIVINE PIZZA

271 Main St, Falmouth, 508-548-1222
www.divinepizza.com
CUISINE: Pizza
DRINKS: Full Bar
SERVING: Lunch, Dinner
PRICE RANGE: $$

This casual pizza joint offers hand-tossed thin-crust pizza, pastas, and sandwiches. The Neopolitan pizza is a favorite. Nice wine list and selection of regional craft beers.

## SIR CRICKET'S FISH & CHIPS

38 Rte 6A, Orleans, 508-255-4453
https://nausetfishandlobsterpool.com/sir-crickets-fish-n-chips

CUISINE: Seafood
DRINKS: No booze
SERVING: Lunch and dinner daily.
PRICE RANGE: $$
Seafood shack with all the usual suspects: platters and rolls of fried clams, scallops, oysters, shrimp.

**SPANKY'S CLAM SHACK**
138 Ocean St #115, Hyannis Port, 508-771-2770
www.spankysclamshack.com
CUISINE: Seafood
DRINKS: Full Bar
SERVING: Lunch, Dinner
PRICE RANGE: $$
This casual family-friendly eatery offers a menu of New England seafood standards. Favorites include: Lobster salad and Roasted Atlantic Swordfish. Extensive cocktail menu. Kids menu and gift shop.

**SPINNAKER**
2019 Main St, Brewster, 508-896-7644
www.spincape.com
CUISINE: Italian
DRINKS: Full Bar
SERVING: Dinner, Lunch (Tues – Sat)
PRICE RANGE: $$
NEIGHBORHOOD: Brewster
Casual beachy-chic eatery serving gourmet Italian fare. There are 3 different rooms you can dine in, casual and cozy. Menu picks: Lobster fritters are crispy and delicious with a hot dipping sauce, Chatham mussels are succulent and the dates stuffed with gorgonzola and wrapped in bacon are just about

the best I've ever had. Save room for the brioche bread pudding served with vanilla ice cream.

**SPOON AND SEED**
12 Thornton Dr, Hyannis, 774-470-4634
www.spoonandseed.com
CUISINE: American (Traditional)/Comfort food
DRINKS: No Booze
SERVING: Breakfast/Lunch
PRICE RANGE: $$
NEIGHBORHOOD: Hyannis
Rustic cafe offering a menu of locally sourced American comfort food. Great breakfast options like the Porto-Benny – their jazzed up version of Eggs Benedict. Favorites: Eggs N' Hash. Not your typical diner fare.

**SUNBIRD KITCHEN**
85 Rt 6A, Orleans, 508-237-0354
www.sunbirdprovisions.com

CUISINE: American (New)/Seafood
DRINKS: Full bar
SERVING: Breakfast/Lunch/Dinner; closed Tues
PRICE RANGE: $$
NEIGHBORHOOD: Orleans
Café offering up locally sourced American cuisine with a twist. Favorites: Smoked mozzarella cheese & kimchi and Bass & beans. Hipster crowd.

**SWEET TOMATOES PIZZA**
461 Station Ave, South Yarmouth, 508-394-6054
www.sweettomatoescapecod.com
CUISINE: Pizza
DRINKS: Beer & Wine Only
SERVING: Lunch, Dinner
PRICE RANGE: $$
A popular pizza chain that attracts locals and tourists. Several locations in the area.

**TERRA LUNA**
104 Shore Rd, North Truro, 508-487-1019
https://terralunarestaurant.com
CUISINE: Italian; New American
DRINKS: Full Bar
SERVING: Breakfast, Tue-Sun 7-12; dinner 5-10
PRICE RANGE: $$
Fra Diablo with mussels and shrimp. Romantic setting. Note that it's also open for breakfast. Romantic setting.

**TIKI PORT**
Capetown Plaza, 714 Iyanough Rd, Hyannis Port, 508-771-5220

www.tikiport.com
CUISINE: Chinese
DRINKS: Full Bar
SERVING: Lunch, Dinner
PRICE RANGE: $$
This long-time favorite offers a giant menu of Chinese and Polynesian cuisine. Bar offers tropical drinks from the South Pacific. Luncheon specials. Known as Cape Cod's #1 Chinese restaurant.

**TIN PAN ALLEY**
269 Commercial St, Provincetown, 508-487-1648
www.tinpanalleyptown.com
CUISINE: Seafood, American (New)
DRINKS: Full Bar
SERVING: Lunch & Dinner
PRICE RANGE: $$
Posh eatery in the center of P-town with a creative menu. Overlooks the ocean. Also has patio dining and a lounge (piano bar) with live entertainment from 9 p.m. Has a popular happy hour. Menu favorites include: Scallops with pea risotto and Swordfish with risotto.

**TREVI CAFÉ & WINE BAR**
25 Market St, Mashpee, 508-477-0055
www.trevicafe.com
CUISINE: Contemporary Mediterranean Cuisine
DRINKS: Full Bar
SERVING: Lunch, Dinner
PRICE RANGE: $$
This is a wine bar with a menu of Contemporary Mediterranean cuisine. The bar offers a list of wines

over 250 wines from around the world. Tapas and Vegetarian options.

**TUGBOATS**
11 Arlington St, West Yarmouth, 508-775-6433
www.tugboatscapecod.com
CUISINE: Seafood/American
DRINKS: Full Bar
SERVING: Lunch, Dinner

PRICE RANGE: $$
This family-friendly seafood eatery offers waterfront and deck seating with great marina views. Menu favorites include: Baked Seafood Macaroni & Cheese and Baked Native Sea Scallops. Great desserts like Cape Cod Mud Pie.

**TWENTY-EIGHT ATLANTIC**
Wequassett Resort, 2173 Rte 28, Harwich, 508-430-3000
www.wequassett.com/dining - /twenty-eight/
CUISINE: Seafood
DRINKS: Full Bar
SERVING: Breakfast 7-11; dinner 6-11
PRICE RANGE: $$$
Dressy, so no shorts or flip-flops. One of the more elegant spots on the Cape located in the Wequassett Resort. Large windows overlook Pleasant Bay. Hand-blown chandeliers, nautical etchings. Paella risotto; lobster & mushroom ravioli; halibut, roasted local cod; lobster braised in butter; beef tenderloin poached in port wine.

**VAN RENSSELAER'S RESTAURANT & RAW BAR**
1019 U.S. 6, Wellfleet, 508-349-2127
www.vanrensselaers.com
CUISINE: Seafood
DRINKS: Full Bar
SERVING: Breakfast, Lunch, & Dinner
PRICE RANGE: $$
Popular seafood eatery that also serves breakfast in the summer. Nice varied menu of Cape Cod fare

specializing in fresh seafood. Breakfast in the summer. Dinner with Early Bird specials. Raw Bar.

**VINING'S BISTRO ON MAIN**
593 Main St, Chatham, 508-945-5033
www.bistroonmainchatham.com
CUISINE: American
DRINKS: Full Bar
SERVING: Lunch - weekends, Dinner nightly; closed Mon & Tues
PRICE RANGE: $$$
Restaurateur Steve Vining's latest incarnation, this bistro offers a menu of internationally inspired food. Favorites include: Caramelized Onion Crusted Black Pearl Organic Salmon and Hickory Braised Cider Brined Pork Shank. Great specials.

**WICKED OYSTER**
50 Main St, Wellfleet, 508-349-3455

www.thewickedo.com
CUISINE: Seafood; steaks, chops
DRINKS: Full Bar
SERVING: Breakfast 7:30 to noon; no lunch in season; dinner from 5.
PRICE RANGE: $
Buttermilk waffles for breakfast; nice range of omelets; huevos rancheros. For dinner, check out the oyster tart as a starter. The grilled marinated pork chop here is served over cheesy grits, topped with stewed apples & pears.

**WICKED RESTAURANT & WINE BAR**
35 South St, Mashpee, 508-477-7422
www.wickedrestaurant.com
CUISINE: Pizza/American/Gluten-Free
DRINKS: Full Bar
SERVING: Lunch, Dinner
PRICE RANGE: $$
This stylish eatery offers a creative menu of pizza and American fare. Gluten-free options. Favorites include: Sweet Ginger Soy Grilled Salmon and Fresh Cavatelli Pasta. Impressive wine list.

**WILD GOOSE TAVERN**
512 Main St, Chatham, 508-945-5590
www.wildgoosetavern.com
CUISINE: American
DRINKS: Full Bar
SERVING: Lunch, Dinner
PRICE RANGE: $$
This casual eatery offers a menu of fresh seafood and American cuisine. Impressive selection of

sandwiches, burgers and salads. Favorites include: Chicken & Spinach Burger and Faroe Islands Salmon. Creative cocktail list.

---

**WINSLOW'S TAVERN**
316 Main St, Wellfleet, 508-349-6450
www.winslowstavern.com
CUISINE: American
DRINKS: Full Bar
SERVING: Lunch - weekends, Dinner – nightly; closed Mon
PRICE RANGE: $$

Located in an 1880's mansion, this popular tavern offers a varied menu of New American cuisine and seafood favorites. Favorites include: Tail And Claw Lobster Roll and Grilled Chicken Paillard. Reservations recommended.

**YARDARM**
48 S Orleans Rd, Orleans, 508-255-4840
www.the-yardarm.com
CUISINE: Seafood/American/Pub
DRINKS: Full Bar
SERVING: Lunch, Dinner
PRICE RANGE: $$
A popular hangout for locals and tourists, this eatery offers a menu of American classics and seafood along with bar snacks. Favorites include: Clam strips and BBQ ribs. TVs to watch sports.

**YARMOUTH HOUSE**
335 Massachusetts 28, West Yarmouth, 508-771-5154
www.yarmouthhouse.com
CUISINE: Seafood/Steakhouse
DRINKS: Full Bar
SERVING: Breakfast, Lunch, & Dinner
PRICE RANGE: $$$
Popular dining spot with great views of the water mill. Nice varied menu featuring items like lobster and prime rib. If you're a fan of seafood and steak try the Filet Mignon a la Neptune (lobster on top with hollandaise sauce). Family friendly.

**ZOE'S PIZZA**
38 Bates Rd, Mashpee, 508-477-1711
www.zoespizza.com
CUISINE: Pizza
DRINKS: No Booze
SERVING: Lunch, Dinner
PRICE RANGE: $
Popular pizzeria with a menu of pizzas, calzones, pastas and homemade lasagna. Favorites include their BBQ chicken pizza and the classic Hawaiian pizza.

# INDEX

## B



## C



## D

## M



## N



## O



## P



## R



## S

www.ingramcontent.com/pod-product-compliance
Ingram Content Group UK Ltd.
Pitfield, Milton Keynes, MK11 3LW, UK
UKHW021647190726
13853UKWH00001B/111

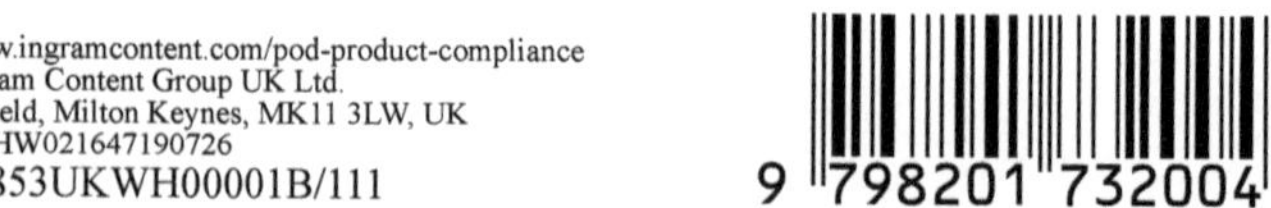

9 798201 732004